Animal Sticker Book

Illustrated by Cecilia Johansson

Contents

There are lots of stickers in the middle
of this book for you to stick on each page.

Words by Jessica Greenwell

Designed by Meg Dobbie and Hanri van Wyk

1

Dusty desert

It's hot and dry in the Australian desert. Where could you put a kangaroo and some hopping mice?

In the farmyard

It's feeding time on the farm. Can you find a place for a hungry horse?

Grassy plains

It's very hot in the African grasslands. Where could you put a muddy hippopotamus?

A snowy world

It's a cold, icy day in the Arctic. Can you put a polar bear on the snow?

Dusty desert – page 2

Kangaroo

Wombat

Possum

Dingo

Parakeet

Emu

Kookaburras

Goanna

Hopping mice

Wallaby

In the farmyard – page 4

Duck

Ducklings

Chicks

Foal

Cow

Hen

Horse

Sheep

Donkey

Hen

Goat

Lambs

Chick

Bull

A snowy world – page 8

Snowy owls

Polar bear cubs

Arctic hare

Arctic foxes

Walruses

Polar bear

Icy waters – page 9

Penguins

Seals

Ice fish

Grassy plains – page 6

Guinea fowl

Dung beetle

Hippopotamuses

Zebras

Gazelle

Cheetah

Leopard

Giraffe

Giraffe

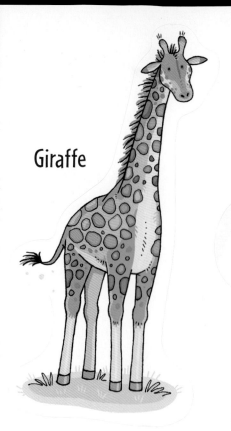

Rhinoceros

Baby elephant

Lion

Lioness

Lion cubs

Ostrich

Elephant

Animals at home

Worm

Birds

Cat

Rabbit

Mole

Frog

Cat

Snail

Mouse

Dog

Puppy

Kitten

Mice

Caterpillar

Guinea pigs

Birds

Bee

In the rainforest – page 12

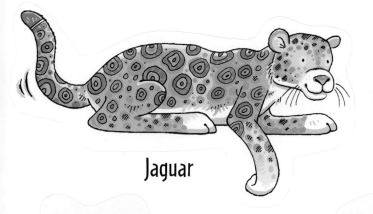

Jaguar

Tapir

Monkey

Butterflies

Sloths

Tree frogs

Alligator

Toucan

Armadillo

Snakes

Parrots

Tree frogs

Under the sea – page 14

Jellyfish

Dolphin

Angelfish

Crab

Sea anemone

Shark

Rainbow fish

Starfish

Sea turtles

Octopus

Dolphin

Squid

Clown fish

Sea horse

Icy waters

In the Antarctic the water is freezing cold. Where could you put a swimming penguin and some ice fish?

Animals at home

Pets love to be outside in the springtime. Can you find a place for a puppy chasing a butterfly?

In the rainforest

The rainforest is full of tall trees and big plants.
Where could you stick a slithering snake?

Under the sea

There are lots of animals in the deep blue sea.
Where could a crab crawl and a sea horse swim?

Baby animal puzzle

Can you help each animal find its baby?